JESUS the REASON

8 studies for individuals or groups

James W. Sire

With Notes for Leaders

InterVarsity Press
Downers Grove, Illinois

OTHER BOOKS BY JAMES W. SIRE

Chris Chrisman Goes to College
Discipleship of the Mind
Habits of the Mind
How to Read Slowly
Naming the Elephant
Scripture Twisting
The Universe Next Door
Václav Havel
Why Should Anyone Believe Anything at All?

InterVarsity Press
P.O. Box 1400, Downers Grove, IL 60515-1426
World Wide Web: www.ivpress.com
E-mail: mail@ivpress.com

Third edition ©1996, 2004 by James W. Sire

Second edition © 1988, revised 1993, and published by Harold Shaw Publishers as Meeting Jesus

InterVarsity Press® is the book-publishing division of InterVarsity Christian Fellowship/USA®, a student movement active on campus at hundreds of universities, colleges and schools of nursing in the United States of America, and a member movement of the International Fellowship of Evangelical Students. For information about local and regional activities, write Public Relations Dept., InterVarsity Christian Fellowship/USA, 6400 Schroeder Rd., P.O. Box 7895, Madison, WI 53707-7895, or visit the IVCF website at <www.ivcf.org>.

LifeGuide® is a registered trademark of InterVarsity Christian Fellowship.

All Scripture quotations, unless otherwise indicated, are taken from the Holy Bible, New International Version®. NIV®. *Copyright ©1973, 1978, 1984 by International Bible Society. Used by permission of Zondervan Publishing House. All rights reserved.*

Cover image: Maynard Owen Williams/National Geographic Cover Image Collection

ISBN 0-8308-3080-4

Printed in the United States of America ∞

P	17	16	15	14	13	12	11	10	9	8	7	6	5	4	3
Y	17	16	15	14	13	12	11	10	09	08	07	06	05		

Contents

Getting the Most Out of *Jesus the Reason*

Jesus is an amazingly attractive, utterly exasperating person. And each of us needs the opportunity to decide what we think of him. This guide is designed to introduce Jesus' character, especially as he interacted with his followers and confronted his enemies and detractors. Jesus came to Israel in the flesh. Now he comes to us in the Gospels.

But why should we take Jesus seriously? Is he not just one of many religious teachers? Why should we pay special attention to him? The answer is clear: he made some startling claims. If they are true, they apply to us as much as to his first disciples. If we are to be honest in our search for truth, we have to take him seriously.

You see, Jesus claimed to have a special insight into who God is. He claimed to act in God's place, forgiving sins and casting out demons—to be so related to God that he could call him *dearest father,* something no one else at that time would ever do. He even thought of himself as the suffering servant of Isaiah 53, the one who would himself be the sacrifice for our sins. He insisted that what he said is so true and so important that our very lives—now and in eternity—are at stake. If we miss him, Jesus said, we miss life itself.

To our ears—and to ancient ones too—this sounds like madness. Surely a person who makes such radical claims is either a liar or a lunatic. So we reason, and so did people in his day. The choice has always been stark: liar, lunatic or Lord. How then do we decide?

Jesus is his own best case for who he is. So "come and see" is the best single approach for a seeker to take (John 1:39, 46). That is what these studies are designed to do.

Suggestions for Individual Study

1. As you begin each study, pray that God will speak to you through his Word.

2. Read the introduction to the study and respond to the personal reflection question or exercise. This is designed to help you focus on God and on the theme of the study.

3. Each study deals with a particular passage—so that you can delve into the author's meaning in that context. Read and reread the passage to be studied. The questions are written using the language of the New International Version, so you may wish to use that version of the Bible. The New Revised Standard Version is also recommended.

4. This is an inductive Bible study, designed to help you discover for yourself what Scripture is saying. The study includes three types of questions. *Observation* questions ask about the basic facts: who, what, when, where and how. *Interpretation* questions delve into the meaning of the passage. *Application* questions help you discover the implications of the text for growing in Christ. These three keys unlock the treasures of Scripture.

Write your answers to the questions in the spaces provided or in a personal journal. Writing can bring clarity and deeper understanding of yourself and of God's Word.

5. It might be good to have a Bible dictionary handy. Use it to look up any unfamiliar words, names or places.

6. Use the prayer suggestion to guide you in thanking God for what you have learned and to pray about the applications that have come to mind.

7. You may want to go on to the suggestion under "Now or Later," or you may want to use that idea for your next study.

Suggestions for Members of a Group Study

1. Come to the study prepared. Follow the suggestions for individual study mentioned above. You will find that careful preparation will greatly enrich your time spent in group discussion.

2. Be willing to participate in the discussion. The leader of your group will not be lecturing. Instead, he or she will be encouraging the members of the group to discuss what they have learned. The leader will be asking the questions that are found in this guide.

3. Stick to the topic being discussed. Your answers should be based on the verses which are the focus of the discussion and not on outside authorities such as commentaries or speakers. These studies focus on a particular passage of Scripture. Only rarely should you refer to other portions of the Bible. This allows for everyone to participate in in-depth study on equal ground.

4. Be sensitive to the other members of the group. Listen attentively when they describe what they have learned. You may be surprised by their insights! Each question assumes a variety of answers. Many questions do not have "right" answers, particularly questions that aim at meaning or application. Instead the questions push us to explore the passage more thoroughly.

When possible, link what you say to the comments of others. Also, be affirming whenever you can. This will encourage some of the more hesitant members of the group to participate.

5. Be careful not to dominate the discussion. We are sometimes so eager to express our thoughts that we leave too little opportunity for others to respond. By all means participate! But allow others to also.

6. Expect God to teach you through the passage being discussed and through the other members of the group. Pray that you will have an enjoyable and profitable time together, but also that as a result of the study you will find ways that you can take action individually and/or as a group.

7. Remember that anything said in the group is considered confidential and should not be discussed outside the group unless specific permission is given to do so.

8. If you are the group leader, you will find additional suggestions at the back of the guide.

1

The Unexpected Jesus

Mark 2:1-12

When a famous person comes to town, many people come to meet that person. They come with expectations, ones that are often belied by the person in person.

GROUP DISCUSSION. Consider this situation. You have heard that a man with great wisdom and healing power is visiting your neighbor down the street. You have been invited to come meet him. What expectations would you have? The family next door has a child with a serious health problem. What might they expect?

PERSONAL REFLECTION. Think back to a time when someone offended you. What needed to happen before a good relationship between the two of you could be restored?

In this passage we will see Jesus handle an awkward situation. He was teaching when suddenly he was interrupted by a demand for his immediate attention. The request was for physical healing, but Jesus focused on something else first. *Read Mark 2:1-12.*

---

1. Imagine yourself as one of those in the house and describe the scene: the kind of people who were there, the room they were in, the events that shattered the calm of the teaching.

---

2. Describe the attitude of the paralytic and the four men as they came to Jesus (vv. 3-5).

---

3. When Jesus says that the man's sins are forgiven (v. 5), what do you think must have been the reaction of the man and his friends?

How would you react if the famous healer told you your sins were forgiven?

4. Were the religious leaders justified in reacting as they did (vv. 6-7)? Explain.

5. What answer do you suppose Jesus expected from this question: "Which is easier: to say to the paralytic, 'Your sins are forgiven,' or to say, 'Get up, take your mat and walk'" (v. 9)? Why?

6. Why did Jesus ask the question anyway (v. 10)?

7. Describe the reactions of the crowd.

8. How did Jesus both confirm and upset the expectations people of his day had about him?

9. How, if at all, has your understanding of Jesus changed through the study of this event in Jesus' life?

Reflect on the implications of Jesus' claim to forgive sins. If you have experienced this personally, thank him now in prayer.

Now or Later

Reflect on these biblical passages that speak of God's forgiveness: Isaiah 1:18; 1 John 1:8-10 and Romans 5:6-8. What is Jesus' role in forgiving sins?

2

Jesus the Lover of Sinners

Luke 7:36-50

The best class of people hangs out with only the best class of people. Right? After all, as the Earl of Chesterfield once said, you tend to "take the tone of the company you are in."

But Jesus surprised normal society. He had a way of upsetting the normal social expectations, making some more at ease and others more frustrated. He changed those considered outcasts into the best of company. And he called the respected religious leaders hypocrites. This passage helps us to imagine what it would have been like to be a guest at a dinner party with Jesus.

GROUP DISCUSSION. Imagine that you are invited to a class reunion. When you arrive, you notice a lot of people who have no connection whatsoever to your class. Some have obviously crashed the party. How would you feel?

PERSONAL REFLECTION. You have offended your friend Ruth. Deeply sorry for this, you go to a friend's house to see her. When you get a chance to speak to her what would you say?

Read Luke 7:36-50.

1. Put yourself in the position of one of the Pharisees watching what takes place in verses 36-38. What would seem unusual about what you are observing?

2. What assumptions is Simon making about the woman and about Jesus (v. 39)?

3. At this point in the story, who do you most identify with— Simon or the woman? Why?

4. Jesus seems to know what Simon is thinking (v. 39). Why do you suppose Jesus responded with a story?

5. How does Jesus explain the woman's actions (vv. 44-48)?

6. What does Jesus want Simon to conclude about the woman and about him?

7. How does this passage fulfill what Isaiah prophesied about Jesus (Luke 4:18-19)?

8. This passage says much about sin. Who can have their sins forgiven?

9. What is required of sinners before they can be forgiven?

Think about an action or attitude (or many of them) for which you really want forgiveness. Ask God for that in prayer.

Now or Later

If you have asked Jesus to forgive you for the thing you have been thinking about, now imagine him saying, "Your sins are forgiven," just as he said to the woman at Simon's house (v. 48).

Consider how you will show your gratitude and love for God. Write down your thoughts and begin to act on them.

3

The Sin
Jesus Forgives

Mark 7:1-23

For some of us the word *sin* has lost its sting. "After all," we say, "we're all sinners. What's so bad about that?" Or *sin* is pooh-poohed as the out-of-date language of straight-laced kill-joys who'll say anything to take the fun out of life.

GROUP DISCUSSION. When the word *sin* comes up in conversation, what sparks the conversation, and what does it usually seem to mean?

PERSONAL REFLECTION. When you think back on your life, what actions have you performed or thoughts have you had that seem especially unworthy to you, let alone to God? Do you think of them as sin or just really bad mistakes?

When Jesus faced the paralytic in Mark 2:1-12, it was sin he dealt with first. And when he forgave the woman of the street, she lavished her love on him. What is sin anyway? *Read Mark 7:1-23.*

---

1. Describe the different groups mentioned in the passage.

---

2. How did the issue of sin arise (vv. 1-5)?

---

3. Why do you suppose Jesus' reply to the religious leaders was so harsh?

---

4. What does the quotation from Isaiah 29:13 in verses 6-7 add to Jesus' own words?

5. What illustration does Jesus give of the Pharisees' hypocrisy (v. 9)? What hypocrisies might Jesus notice among religious leaders today?

6. What illustrations might Jesus use if he were to address our culture or, better, your church or fellowship group?

7. According to Jesus, what makes a person unclean (vv. 15-20)?

What does this tell us about human nature—what we are and what we need to become?

8. Some of the sins listed in verses 21-22 are actions, some are attitudes. Some seem major, others minor. Why do you think Jesus neither notes these differences nor ranks the sins?

9. Considering the panoramic sweep of the list of sins in verses 21-22, how would you go about demonstrating to yourself that you were not a sinner?

Think about your own everyday habits and encounters. How can you receive God's forgiveness and begin to live a life worthy of Jesus?

Now or Later

This passage itself seems not to contain any "good news." How is this bad news countered by what we have learned about Jesus in Mark 2:1-12 and Luke 7:36-50?

4

Jesus
the Good Teacher

Luke 10:25-37

Jesus taught by telling stories. We all know that. But do we know just how clever these stories were? In this study we look at one of his most famous parables, focusing not only on the moral of the story but also on how the story makes it known.

GROUP DISCUSSION. We should help our neighbors; that is a principle most of us try to live by. But who are our neighbors? That is, how far afield are we to go from our home turf?

PERSONAL REFLECTION. You have very limited resources of time and money. How do you decide who to help?

Read Luke 10:25-37.

1. What do you learn about the expert in the law from verse 25?

2. What makes the first question asked by the "expert in the law" so important (v. 25)?

3. Why do you suppose Jesus answered a question with a question (v. 26)?

4. What does the lawyer's answer and Jesus' response show about the lawyer's understanding (vv. 27-28)? (See Deuteronomy 6:5 and Leviticus 19:18.)

5. How would you react if Jesus had told you to keep the great commandments of loving God and neighbor in order to have eternal life?

6. In the story Jesus tells in verses 30-35, what kinds of people failed to help the man?

7. Jews and Samaritans, like some Catholics and Protestants in Northern Ireland, were openly hostile toward one another. Why is the Samaritan such an unlikely hero in a story told by a Jew to a Jew?

8. What point(s) is Jesus making in choosing the Samaritan as "neighbor"?

9. If you were the lawyer, an expert in the interpretation of the Torah (the first five books of the Hebrew Scriptures), how would you feel about Jesus' answer?

---

10. What insight into Jesus' character—who he was, who he thought he was—does this encounter with the lawyer reveal?

Ask God to reveal to you the hidden flaws in your character, and pray not just for his forgiveness but also for a change in your own inner being.

Now or Later

Consider the ways in which Jesus, while not answering the question the lawyer asked, introduced the lawyer to a truth he would never have seen on his own. How did Jesus' story engage and challenge the life of the lawyer?

5

Jesus and the Father

What is God like? Is he the vengeful God who pours out wrath on all who cross him? Or is he a cuddly bear who always gives out warm fuzzies?

GROUP DISCUSSION. What is your picture of God?

PERSONAL REFLECTION. Do you have any friends that your closest friends think you shouldn't be hanging out with? Or is there a time when you have done this in the past? Why do you do this?

Jesus tells a story that trumpets one very important side of God's character. In Luke this parable is one of three Jesus told in response to the stringent religious leaders of his day who complained that Jesus "welcomes sinners and eats with them" (Luke 15:2). That setting becomes important as we look at just what Jesus' most famous parable means. *Read Luke 15:11-32.*

---

1. How would you characterize the younger son from verses 12-16?

---

2. Pigs were considered unclean by the Jews; feeding them and desiring their food would be particularly unappealing to this son. Why did he decide to return home (v. 17)?

---

3. What did he hope his father would do (vv. 18-19)?

---

4. What does the reaction of the father to his returning son tell us about the father's character (vv. 20-24)?

5. Why does the father immediately call for a feast (vv. 24, 32)?

_____

6. Why does the older son reject his father's acceptance of his younger brother?

_____

7. Why do you think Jesus ended the story of the older son before the son makes his final decision to stay in the field or go in to the feast?

_____

8. Recall that this parable was told to the Pharisees who complained about who Jesus associated with (Luke 15:2). Where might they have seen themselves in the story?

_____

9. In defending his eating with sinners, what is Jesus claiming for himself?

10. Define the concept of repentance using only this passage (vv. 11-32) as an illustration. What role in the concept is played by each of the three principal characters?

Each of us is or at one time has been one of the sons in this parable. Which son in the parable do you best understand? What does Jesus offer you?

Now or Later

Write your own version of this parable, choosing characters who act in the same way but do so in a twenty-first-century context. Share it with the group at a later time.

6

Jesus the Servant and Savior

Mark 10:32-45

"What would you like to be when you grow up?" we ask our children. We expect them to say something like a firefighter, a police officer, the president, a superhero. We don't expect them to say a waiter, dishwasher, ditchdigger, bank teller or hospital aide. How about you? What would you most like to be?

GROUP DISCUSSION. Imagine a friend of yours asking you to join him or her in a trip to one of the most dangerous spots in the world—say, Iraq—in order to help in relief efforts. How would you respond?

PERSONAL REFLECTION. You are independently wealthy and have a choice between being the leader of a prestigious group and working as a volunteer in a nursing home. Which do you choose to do and why?

Read Mark 10:32-45.

1. Imagine yourself as one of Jesus' followers. You have been with him for a couple of years in Galilee and have seen how he has angered the religious authorities, especially those from headquarters in Jerusalem. How would you feel about going to Jerusalem at a festival time when the city would be filled with many of Jesus' enemies?

2. How would you explain the reason for the astonishment and fear of the disciples and others who were on their way to Jerusalem (vv. 32-34)?

3. Why do you suppose Jesus drew his twelve closest disciples aside to talk with them (v. 32)?

4. After hearing Jesus' words in verses 33-34, how would you view the request made by James and John (vv. 35-37)?

5. Why does Jesus answer them with the question, "Can you drink the cup I drink or be baptized with the baptism I am baptized with" (v. 38)?

What should have been their answer?

---

6. What do Jesus' words in verse 39 really predict about the future of James and John?

---

7. What is the significance of Jesus' teaching in verses 43-44 for people today who believe in Jesus?

What is the significance for those who are still considering whether to follow Jesus?

8. How is the teaching of verses 43-44 worked out in Jesus' life?

9. Jesus' comment that he came "to give his life as a ransom for many" (v. 45) is one of his most explicit explanations of the reason for his life and death. What does the phrase mean?

10. In verse 45 Jesus clearly seems to have had in mind the Servant Song of Isaiah 52:13—53:12, especially Isaiah 53:5 and 10. What sort of person other than one telling the truth would associate himself with the suffering servant of Isaiah?

Thank Jesus for being the ransom for our sins, and ask him to open your heart to being a servant.

Now or Later

Reflect on your own aims and goals for life. Knowing what Jesus said to James and John, consider what he might well say to you were you to ask him to aid you in your pursuit of those goals. Ask God to transform your goals to his goals for you.

7

Jesus the Sacrifice

Mark 14—15

Crosses and crucifixes are present everywhere. They not only adorn church steeples but also are displayed in our homes, hung around our necks and dangled from our ears. They mark the graves of millions of people around the world. Soon after Jesus' death the cross became the central symbol of the Christian faith. The cross reminds us that Jesus died the most despicable death possible. But we see it as a badge of honor.

GROUP DISCUSSION. Why do you think people today still display and wear the cross?

PERSONAL REFLECTION. When you see a cross displayed publicly, what, if anything, comes to mind? Reflect on why you have this response or lack of response.

This study focuses on five events from the last week of Jesus' life. We begin with a brief account of the Last Supper, a Passover feast celebrated by Jesus and his closest disciples. The feast is held in remembrance of the deliverance of Israel from bondage in Egypt (Exodus 12). *Read Mark 14:12-26.*

1. How does Jesus understand the significance of the bread and wine consumed during the feast?

2. *Read Mark 14:32-42.* Every one of us has to face death. Jesus was surely stronger than any of us. Yet many who know they are going to die are far less troubled than Jesus. Why was Jesus so disturbed? (See also Mark 10:45.)

3. *Read Mark 14:53-65.* This is the first of two trials Mark records, this one before the Jewish court, the other before Pilate (15:1-15). What charges were brought against Jesus in Mark 14:53-60?

Which of them is (are) true or the closest to being true?

4. What does Jesus believe about who he is (14:61-62)?

5. *Read Mark 15:1-15.* Why is Pilate concerned with a different charge against Jesus (15:2)?

6. What strikes you about Jesus' demeanor during the trials?

7. *Read Mark 15:21-40.* Why did Jesus not do as he was challenged to do—come down from the cross and save himself (15:30)?

8. Why do you think Jesus cried out from the cross, "My God, my God, why have you forsaken me" (15:33-34)?

9. The centurion guarding the cross exclaimed, "Surely this man was the Son of God" (15:39). Considering all the things we have learned about Jesus over the past seven studies, do you think this conclusion is justified? Explain.

Come to Jesus and thank him for the love expressed in his death on the cross for our sins. Or, if you have not yielded your life to Jesus, do so now.

Now or Later

Review all of the studies to this point and fix in your mind the flow of the argument. The Jesus you have been seeing in Scripture was either who he said and thought he was or he was an impostor, a liar or a very dangerous megalomaniac who has offered a fake salvation. Think about it: Was Jesus a liar, a lunatic or the very Lord of the Universe?

8

The Resurrection of Jesus

Luke 24:1-43

When the apostle Paul mentioned the resurrection of Jesus to the philosophers in Athens, some of them sneered. And well they might! Some still do. After all, such a thing just couldn't happen.

Or could it?

The united testimony of the first disciples, the apostle Paul and the four Gospels is that indeed it did happen. Paul even argues (1 Corinthians 15) that the whole of Christian faith hinges on its happening. Our picture of Jesus would not be complete without seeing his death lead to his resurrection. In this study we will look at some of the evidence.

GROUP DISCUSSION. A short time after C. S. Lewis died, J. B. Phillips suddenly saw Lewis sitting in a chair looking quite alive. How would you react if something like this happened to you after a good friend's death?

PERSONAL REFLECTION. Bring to mind a time of grief. Ask God to allow the joy and hope of Jesus' story to heal any pain you still feel over that loss.

Read Luke 24:1-12.

1. Women were first to visit the tomb. What do you suppose their first reaction was?

2. Given the first-century opinion that the testimony of women was not worth much, why do you think Luke mentions them (v. 1)?

3. Why does the first explanation of the empty tomb make sense to the women (vv. 4-7)?

4. What was the reaction of the disciples, Peter in particular (vv. 9-12)?

5. Note the details about the grave clothes in John 20:3-9. What is the significance of this?

6. *Read Luke 24:13-43.* What did the two disciples reveal about their hopes for Jesus (vv. 19-24)?

7. How would you feel if you had been one of his disciples and had witnessed his crucifixion?

8. Why do you suppose Jesus taught them out of the Scriptures (the Old Testament) (vv. 25-27)?

9. How did the encounter with Jesus affect the two disciples (vv. 31-35)?

10. What is the value of the evidence for the resurrection given in verses 37-43?

---

11. How is the resurrection consistent with the character of Jesus and the claims we have seen him make in the previous studies?

---

12. To summarize, list the kinds of evidence that are given for the resurrection. How does this consideration of the case for the resurrection help confirm you in your faith in Christ or challenge you in your hesitancy to believe?

Praise God for Jesus' victory over the grave, and thank him for the hope that gives us for the future, both here on earth and in heaven.

Now or Later

Given what you have learned about the Lord Jesus Christ, how will you now live your life? List some changes that you have already put into effect. List some you have yet to realize. Thank Jesus for his risen life and your access to him through prayer.

Seeking and Finding God's Forgiveness

If you are not sure that you are in a right relationship with God through the forgiveness of your sins, you can remove that uncertainty now. You can become one of God's children.

I would urge anyone who wishes to come to God to read and study the following prayer. If you believe it expresses your deepest desire, make this prayer your own and pray it quietly and aloud to God.

Heavenly Father, I know that without you I am dead in sin. I am not naturally alive. I am not naturally your child. I know that I put myself first and do not love you as I should or obey your commandments as I should. I know that because of this I do not deserve your love or forgiveness. I deserve to be separated from you forever.

I also know that Jesus Christ, your Son, has died for me. He has paid my penalty of death. I believe in him and place my trust in him.

And so I give myself to you as much as I know how and accept Jesus not only as my Savior but also as my Lord. I want to follow you all the days of my life and so to find life in you throughout eternity.

Please accept me as one of your children and live in me by your Holy Spirit.

In the name of Jesus Christ, amen.

There is no magic in this or any other prayer. Praying it without meaning it, praying it without following through and acting like a child of God, will not merit anything. You may even be in worse condition because you may think this prayer has somehow earned you a place with God.

Nothing earns you life with God. Only God can give this life, and he gives it only to those who are serious about their faith. No one can fool around with God.

But—and what a tremendous *but* it is—John the Gospel writer has great words of encouragement to those who have received Jesus as their Savior and Lord: "To all who received him, to those who believed in his name, he gave the right to become children of God" (John 1:12).

Jesus is our Lord and Savior. We are his children, not because we willed it, but because he did! God is our Father because he wants to be. Praise God!

Leader's Notes

Leading a Bible discussion can be an enjoyable and rewarding experience. This is especially true of the present study, which is designed to be used not only with groups of Christians but groups that include those who have yet to place their trust in Jesus as Savior and Lord.

If as a leader you are using this guide in an investigative Bible study mostly for seekers or new believers, you will want to choose a time convenient to your friends and acquaintances. Then invite them to spend time with you looking at the life of Jesus. Ask a couple of your mature Christian friends to join you for support.

The studies are designed to last less than an hour. In your invitation emphasize that you will be looking together at what the Bible says about Jesus. No one will preach.

It will become obvious as the studies proceed that one cannot forever hold Jesus at a distance. He is always upsetting our expectations and calling us to a commitment that costs us control over our own lives. But let this come out in the studies. As a leader, you do not need to underline the cost of truly believing in Jesus. The Holy Spirit through the biblical text itself will do that. You should, however, be aware that some participants may be undergoing personal struggle. Your task will be to help them come to terms with the Jesus they meet. You may be able to help some to make a commitment to Jesus (see "Seeking and Finding God's Forgiveness," pp. 41-42).

Those who have already come to faith in Christ may struggle as well, for all of us find our understanding of Jesus shattered by fresh study of the Gospels. Pray together that your deepened understanding of Jesus will result in a fuller Christian life. That is a prayer that can be prayed in great confidence of a positive answer.

Because of the intense focus of this study on just a handful of key issues, the leader's notes to each study should be carefully considered before the group meets. This is especially true of studies 1, 2 and 7.

Preparing for the Study

1. Ask God to help you understand and apply the passage in your own life. Unless this happens, you will not be prepared to lead others. Pray too for the various members of the group. Ask God to open your hearts to the message of his Word and motivate you to action.

2. Read the introduction to the entire guide to get an overview of the entire book and the issues which will be explored.

3. As you begin each study, read and reread the assigned Bible passage to familiarize yourself with it.

4. This study guide is based on the New International Version of the Bible. It will help you and the group if you use this translation as the basis for your study and discussion.

5. Carefully work through each question in the study. Spend time in meditation and reflection as you consider how to respond.

6. Write your thoughts and responses in the space provided in the study guide. This will help you to express your understanding of the passage clearly.

7. It might help to have a Bible dictionary handy. Use it to look up any unfamiliar words, names or places. (For additional help on how to study a passage, see chapter five of *How to Lead a LifeGuide Bible Study*, InterVarsity Press.)

8. Consider how you can apply the Scripture to your life. Remember that the group will follow your lead in responding to the studies. They will not go any deeper than you do.

9. Once you have finished your own study of the passage, familiarize yourself with the leader's notes for the study you are leading. These are designed to help you in several ways. First, they tell you the purpose the study guide author had in mind when writing the study. Take time to think through how the study questions work together to

accomplish that purpose. Second, the notes provide you with additional background information or suggestions on group dynamics for various questions. This information can be useful when people have difficulty understanding or answering a question. Third, the leader's notes can alert you to potential problems you may encounter during the study.

10. If you wish to remind yourself of anything mentioned in the leader's notes, make a note to yourself below that question in the study.

Leading the Study

1. Begin the study on time. If it will not put off nonbelievers in the group, open with prayer, asking God to help the group to understand and apply the passage.

2. Be sure that everyone in your group has a study guide. Encourage the group to prepare beforehand for each discussion by reading the introduction to the guide and by working through the questions in the study.

3. At the beginning of your first time together, explain that these studies are meant to be discussions, not lectures. Encourage the members of the group to participate. However, do not put pressure on those who may be hesitant to speak during the first few sessions. You may want to suggest the following guidelines to your group.

☐ Stick to the topic being discussed.

☐ Your responses should be based on the verses which are the focus of the discussion and not on outside authorities such as commentaries or speakers.

☐ These studies focus on a particular passage of Scripture. Only rarely should you refer to other portions of the Bible. This allows for everyone to participate in in-depth study on equal ground.

☐ Anything said in the group is considered confidential and will not be discussed outside the group unless specific permission is given to do so.

☐ We will listen attentively to each other and provide time for each person present to talk.

☐ We will pray for each other.

4. Have a group member read the introduction at the beginning of the discussion.

5. Every session begins with a group discussion question. The question or activity is meant to be used before the passage is read. The question introduces the theme of the study and encourages group members to begin to open up. Encourage as many members as possible to participate, and be ready to get the discussion going with your own response.

This section is designed to reveal where our thoughts or feelings need to be transformed by Scripture. That is why it is especially important not to read the passage before the discussion question is asked. The passage will tend to color the honest reactions people would otherwise give because they are, of course, supposed to think the way the Bible does.

You may want to supplement the group discussion question with an icebreaker to help people to get comfortable. See the community section of *Small Group Idea Book* for more ideas.

You also might want to use the personal reflection question with your group. Either allow a time of silence for people to respond individually or discuss it together.

6. Have a group member (or members if the passage is long) read aloud the passage to be studied. Then give people several minutes to read the passage again silently so that they can take it all in.

7. Question 1 will generally be an overview question designed to briefly survey the passage. Encourage the group to look at the whole passage, but try to avoid getting sidetracked by questions or issues that will be addressed later in the study.

8. As you ask the questions, keep in mind that they are designed to be used just as they are written. You may simply read them aloud. Or you may prefer to express them in your own words.

There may be times when it is appropriate to deviate from the study guide. For example, a question may have already been answered. If so, move on to the next question. Or someone may raise an important question not covered in the guide. Take time to discuss it, but try to keep the group from going off on tangents.

9. Avoid answering your own questions. If necessary, repeat or re-

phrase them until they are clearly understood. Or point out something you read in the leader's notes to clarify the context or meaning. An eager group quickly becomes passive and silent if they think the leader will do most of the talking.

10. Don't be afraid of silence. People may need time to think about the question before formulating their answers.

11. Don't be content with just one answer. Ask, "What do the rest of you think?" or "Anything else?" until several people have given answers to the question.

12. Acknowledge all contributions. Try to be affirming whenever possible. Never reject an answer. If it is clearly off-base, ask, "Which verse led you to that conclusion?" or again, "What do the rest of you think?"

13. Don't expect every answer to be addressed to you, even though this will probably happen at first. As group members become more at ease, they will begin to truly interact with each other. This is one sign of healthy discussion.

14. Don't be afraid of controversy. It can be very stimulating. If you don't resolve an issue completely, don't be frustrated. Move on and keep it in mind for later. A subsequent study may solve the problem.

15. Periodically summarize what the group has said about the passage. This helps to draw together the various ideas mentioned and gives continuity to the study. But don't preach.

16. At the end of the Bible discussion you may want to allow group members a time of quiet to work on an idea under "Now or Later." Then discuss what you experienced. Or you may want to encourage group members to work on these ideas between meetings. Give an opportunity during the session for people to talk about what they are learning.

17. Conclude your time together with conversational prayer, adapting the prayer suggestion at the end of the study to your group. Ask for God's help in following through on the commitments you've made.

18. End on time.

Many more suggestions and helps are found in *How to Lead a LifeGuide Bible Study.*

Components of Small Groups

A healthy small group should do more than study the Bible. There are four components to consider as you structure your time together.

Nurture. Small groups help us to grow in our knowledge and love of God. Bible study is the key to making this happen and is the foundation of your small group.

Community. Small groups are a great place to develop deep friendships with other Christians. Allow time for informal interaction before and after each study. Plan activities and games that will help you get to know each other. Spend time having fun together—going on a picnic or cooking dinner together.

Worship and prayer. Your study will be enhanced by spending time praising God together in prayer or song. Pray for each other's needs—and keep track of how God is answering prayer in your group. Ask God to help you to apply what you are learning in your study.

Outreach. Reaching out to others can be a practical way of applying what you are learning, and it will keep your group from becoming self-focused. Host a series of evangelistic discussions for your friends or neighbors. Clean up the yard of an elderly friend. Serve at a soup kitchen together, or spend a day working on a Habitat house.

Many more suggestions and helps in each of these areas are found in *Small Group Idea Book.* Information on building a small group can be found in *Small Group Leaders' Handbook* and *The Big Book on Small Groups* (both from InterVarsity Press). Reading through one of these books would be worth your time.

Study 1. The Unexpected Jesus. Mark 2:1-12.

Purpose: To show that Jesus surprised those of his day both by the extraordinary way he lived his life and by seeing himself as a person with a divine nature and a divine mission.

General note. Jesus' claim to forgive sins is a key element in his self-understanding, for if he thought he could forgive sins, he was taking onto himself an ability God alone could have. Thus he was implicitly claiming either to be divine or to be acting on behalf of God. No good Jew—rabbi, scholar or ordinary person—would do that.

Group discussion. You may wish to alter this question by identifying the person as a celebrity—say, Paul Simon or Shirley MacLaine for the older set, or Sean Penn or the Dixie Chicks for the younger. The point is to acknowledge the difference between image and reality.

Personal reflection. This could also be used by the group. It raises a key issue in Jesus' teaching and his actions: Who can forgive sins and thus restore the relationship between individuals and God?

Question 2. The idea here is to set in the mind of the participants the drama of the events.

Question 4. This is a speculative question, but the presumption is that they all wanted a physical cure and would have been surprised at Jesus' declaration.

Question 5. The Pharisees were a religious sect of Jews bent on a strict interpretation of the Law, and most teachers of the law were Pharisees. It stands to reason that they would be upset, and since Jesus knew the Law very well (and could probably see angry looks on their faces), we can be sure he knew exactly what they would think even before he spoke. Actually, the reaction of the religious leaders is well founded. Only the one offended can forgive the offending one. When Jesus says that the man's sins (offenses against God) are forgiven, he is making an implicit claim to divinity. Only God could make such a declaration.

Make sure you discuss the issue of forgiveness. Who has to do the forgiving? If participants have trouble coming to the conclusion that only the offended party can forgive the offender, have them think of a person they have offended. Then say to them, "Hey, it's okay. I forgive you for what you did to that person." Are they forgiven? Of course not! Discuss, too, how even if the offender apologizes or agrees to pay for the damage, a person is not obligated to forgive him or her. The act of forgiveness comes from the heart of the offended person as an act of undeserved favor.

Question 6. Anyone could *say* either one. It is the *doing* of either that is the difficult task. One can, of course, be observed; the other cannot.

Question 7. If he can heal the paralytic—that is, act as a physical healer—there is reason to believe that he can also act as a spiritual healer.

Question 9. The people in this passage came from a wide spectrum of Jewish society: religious leaders, ordinary Galileans, the poor, the wealthy, the needy and the curious. (See the list in the parallel passage in Luke 5:17.) Their expectations would differ, but it is clear from Mark 1 that many would expect him to be a teacher or prophet (not so much that he would foretell the future but that he would call people to obedience to the Law or to a special style of life); they also expected him to be a healer and perhaps worker of other wonders. They would not expect him to claim to forgive sins.

The answers given here are a preface to the key question of all the studies: Who is Jesus? The studies that follow continue to help flesh out the character and teaching of Jesus, especially as it relates to our relation to him, to the Father and to the Holy Spirit.

Prayer. Use these suggestions as it seems appropriate and comfortable to your context. It may be more comfortable for seekers if you or one of the other Christians in your group prays aloud for everyone. You may also find that in time the seekers in the group become comfortable praying as well.

Now or Later. Reflect on these biblical passages. This study and subsequent studies as well may prompt some in the group to wonder if their own sins have been forgiven. Some may wish at this point to seek God's forgiveness. Suggest that they turn to "Seeking and Finding God's Forgiveness" on pages 41-42 to guide them in their way.

Study 2. Jesus the Lover of Sinners. Luke 7:36-50.

Purpose: To show Jesus' compassion for sinners. There is no sinner so sinful that repentance is not possible.

Personal reflection. This reflection is probably best not used with the group. It probes into deep feelings.

Question 1. Jesus would have been reclining, as was the custom at formal dinners. That the woman was there at all is amazing; that Jesus would allow her to touch him is stranger yet.

Question 2. Simon as a strict Pharisee assumes that prophets would not associate with social outcasts, especially women of the street.

Question 3. People in the group may not wish to be honest about who they side with. This may come out in the discussion. Keep the discussion short and don't let people draw final conclusions yet.

Question 4. Jesus often taught in parables—clever stories designed to uncover a truth, often a truth about the person to whom Jesus was speaking. Try discussing how we are often more willing to believe what someone is teaching us if we are involved in the process. Here Jesus involves Simon in the judgment about the quality of love forgiven sinners can be expected to display.

Question 5. Jesus says the woman loves him because he has forgiven her sins. Apparently the woman has met Jesus before and he has already forgiven her sins. She has now sought him out to express her appreciation. At the end of the dialogue, then, Jesus reassures here of that forgiveness (v. 48). This question can be used as an application question to help participants see *how* Jesus is making his point about who is accepted by God.

Question 6. He wants Simon to see that the woman has been forgiven and that Simon has not. Only the ones who recognize their own sin can be forgiven. Simon does not recognize his own sin. This is a condition worse than that of the woman, whose sins are so obvious to Simon and society at large. Simon should grasp that in Jesus' estimation it is Simon who is the outcast and the woman who is welcomed into God's kingdom.

Question 7. The woman is not monetarily poor (she has a flask of expensive perfume), but she has been a prisoner of her profession and Jesus has set her free.

Question 8. Anyone can have his or her sins forgiven.

Question 9. Repentance—sorrow for sin and turning away from its practice—is the only requirement.

Prayer. If participants pray during group time, do not require them to be specific about their sins unless they want to. Some who are just learning about Jesus may be overcome with emotion as they reflect on this passage. Some may be so troubled by guilt for past sins that this passage leads them to repentance and acceptance of Jesus as their Savior. Be prepared to help anyone who would like to do that. One good way to do this is to refer them to "Seeking and Finding God's Forgiveness" on pages 41-42.

Study 3. The Sin Jesus Forgives. Mark 7:1-23.

Purpose: To understand what Jesus taught about the primary reason we are at odds with God.

Group discussion. Be careful not to let your group get bogged down in a discussion about *which* things are actually *sins*. The point here is to notice how people react to sin in general: Do they ignore it? Do they laugh about it? Are they uncomfortable, or do they speak out against it?

Question 3. Jesus is always harder on the self-righteous than on the sinners who know they are sinners (recall Simon in Lk 7:36-50).

Question 4. It grounds Jesus' teaching in the very tradition they thought they were upholding and shows Jesus' respect for that tradition. The problem, then, was not what the Scriptures teach but with how they were being distorted.

Question 5. The term *Corban* means money devoted to God by an oath. Though respect for parents was at the heart of the law, a selfish son could promise the temple the money that would normally have been given for the care of parents, and so avoid his duty.

Question 6. Don't spend a lot of time on this. Illustrations should be easily forthcoming.

Question 7. If evil comes from the inside, then human beings are evil at heart. The romantic notion that all we have to do to become good is to get rid of the evil influences in our lives (through, say, some regimen of meditation) is clearly false. We must be forgiven for who we are, not just for what we have done. And we need to be transformed in character as well so that we can act out of good and not evil inclinations.

Question 8. In the final analysis all sin is sin and has as a consequence: our separation from God. See James 2:8-11.

Question 9. The only way to demonstrate to yourself that you are not a sinner is to lie to yourself. The apostle Paul put the same point this way: "For all have sinned and fall short of the glory of God" (Rom 3:23).

Now or Later. It may help for someone in the group to summarize what has been learned earlier about forgiveness in studies 1 and 2. Some may be so troubled by guilt for past sins that this passage leads them to repentance and acceptance of Jesus as their Savior. Be prepared to help anyone who would like to do that. One good way to do this is to refer them to "Seeking and Finding God's Forgiveness" on pages 41-42.

Study 4. Jesus the Good Teacher. Luke 10:25-37.
Purpose: To show the clever way Jesus taught and thus to heighten the contrast needed for the trilemma: Jesus as liar, lunatic or Lord.
Group discussion. This study takes a risk. The opening discussion focuses on the same question that the "expert in the law" asked Jesus. It got the lawyer in deep trouble. He discovered it was the wrong question to ask. So as you begin this study, treat the members in your group with some compassion, for that first question leads them astray. All their calculations of just how far afield one might go to find a neighbor is couched in the rhetoric of the kingdom of darkness. When the light dawns on them, they may be angry with you or this guide. So proceed with caution! Let participants air their views and argue a bit with each other if they disagree; then gently ask them to take a look at what happened when the lawyer asked Jesus the same question.
Question 2. The question is important because it focuses on the longing each person has for continued existence. Few like to contemplate their fate after death, especially if they have no confidence in their own eternal destiny.
Question 3. It requires the questioner to become involved in the answer to his own question.
Question 4. Jesus himself summed up the commandments in similar terms in Mark 12:28-34 (see Deut 6:5 and Lev 19:18). So the lawyer understood the essence of the law.
Question 5. This application question is designed to bring out the dilemma faced by the lawyer. He knew what to do, but he also knew he was not doing it. So he tried to dodge the issue by getting Jesus to define *neighbor* in a way that he could in some way obey.
Question 6. The priest and Levite (a member of a lesser order of temple officials) represent those in society who are thought to be and generally claim to be righteous.

Question 7. Samaritans were cousins to the Israelites but were not accepted on even terms. In fact, Jews did not associate with Samaritans (Jn 4:9). Ask participants what the modern counterparts to Samaritans are today—in, say, Israel, Croatia, Belfast and so on.

Question 8. Help participants to see that Jesus shows that the lawyer's question is the wrong one. Righteousness in God's eyes is not to be determined that way. The real issue is not "Who is my neighbor?" but "Will I be a neighbor?"

Questions 9-10. The intent of these questions is to get participants to realize just how wise and powerful Jesus shows himself to be. He is not a person we can manipulate with our questions or dodge with our deceptive answers. He knows us too well for that. We must deal with him as he is, not as we wish him to be.

At the end of the study, you may wish to have someone answer the central question of all the studies: As we have seen him so far, what kind of person is Jesus showing himself to be?

Study 5. Jesus and the Father. Luke 15:11-32.

Purpose: To show that God as Father accepts those who know themselves to be sinners and that Jesus sees himself as standing in the place of the Father, acting as the Father acts.

General note. The parable of the prodigal son is deservedly famous. Within its brief compass is displayed a rich insight into the character of God—the longing of God the Father for the lost, his joy at their repentance, his graciousness in forgiving, the lavishness of his response to the repentant. It also shows a profound insight into the human psychology of sin and repentance. Its central message should not be missed: God is waiting to receive his wayward children; they need only recognize their lostness, turn around and come back to him.

Group discussion. It may help to note that the Pharisees had a rule against sharing "table fellowship" with people they considered sinful. Yet Jesus frequently dined with sinners (see Lk 5:30-31 where he explains why).

Question 2. To the Jews, even orthodox Jews today, pigs are unclean animals, not to be raised or eaten.

Question 4. Though the father is well aware of the sinful past of his son, he has a lavish, even overwhelming, abundance of compassion and mercy.

Question 5. Holding a feast was a common way to celebrate—as it still is—and in the Gospels signals the presence of the kingdom of God.

Question 6. The older brother considers himself righteous, but his righteousness is only negative; he has not directly disobeyed his father. The father's righteousness is like God's: it includes mercy and forgiveness (as we saw in the previous study).

Question 7. The older brother can come in to the feast any time he decides to do so, but if he does not, he puts himself outside the father's family. Jesus ended the story here because this story can only be ended by a decision of the older brother. By extension, unless we accept the character of our Father God, we too will put ourselves outside his kingdom. Ending the story here is one of the ways in which Jesus makes this an excellent story. The audience becomes involved in the story; they write the ending.

Question 8. The Pharisees would almost surely see themselves as the older son. They had not left home. They were the guardians of the household. Their complaint that Jesus ate with sinners puts them outside the kingdom of God as Jesus presents and embodies it.

Question 9. Jesus is implying that he and God the Father are one in character and action. Jesus eats with the outcasts. God accepts sinners and forgives them.

Question 10. The father in the story acts like God in accepting repentant sinners (the younger son) and in calling to repentance the unrepentant sinners (the older son who sins in failing to accept his father's forgiving nature). Emphasize the need for God's grace in accepting and forgiving us.

The study ends with the challenge to respond to what Jesus is teaching and showing himself to be. If any participant wishes to repent now, you may get help from "Seeking and Finding God's Forgiveness" (pp. 41-42).

Study 6. Jesus the Servant and Savior. Mark 10:32-45.
Purpose: To show that Jesus understood his death as a ransom for the

sins of the world.

Question 2. The disciples were well aware of the tension that was building around Jesus. Both the religious and political authorities (sometimes the same people) were trying to get rid of him or at least marginalize the impact of his teachings that challenged the established order. To go to the seat of both the religious and political power at a festival time could only mean conflict, perhaps death (Lk 11:31; Jn 11:7-16).

Question 3. The teaching about his death and resurrection was intended only for his closest disciples. It should have prepared them for the tough days ahead.

Question 4. Like most Jews of Jesus' day, the disciples were expecting a political messiah, one who would deliver them from Roman rule. Even his disciples failed to understand when Jesus predicted what would happen in Jerusalem.

Question 5. Jesus calls them to be his full disciples, but it is they who must make the choice. They are ready for what they hope will happen (that he will seize power and deliver Israel from Rome), but in saying they are willing to go through the ordeal he will be going through, they do not understand just what they have agreed to. Given the way they behaved when the cup was offered to them, they should have said no at the outset.

Question 6. Jesus predicts the same persecution for the disciples as he will himself receive. Acts 12:2 tells of the death of James at the hands of Herod. Revelation 1:9 speaks of John's exile and suffering for the sake of Christ.

Question 7. This is an important application question, raising the issue of our willingness to follow Jesus no matter what. We, however, can have a better notion of what might ensue for us as we follow Jesus because we know what he went through. To follow Jesus is to live a life shaped by the prospect, if not the reality, of the cross. For those still considering Christianity for themselves, it brings up the cost of commitment.

Questions 8-9. Question 8 is designed to overview the events; question 9, the meaning—Jesus' death is the sacrifice for our sins. Paul elaborates on the concept in Romans 5:6-9. The meaning of Jesus' death is dealt with in more detail in study 7—see the leader's notes for questions 1 and 3-8. If the group jumps ahead and answers question 9 along with 8, then you can skip question 9 and move to 10.

Question 10. This question raises the issue of Jesus as liar, lunatic or Lord.

Prayer. This discussion and prayer could lead people to ask for Jesus' forgiveness and become committed to him as Lord and Savior. If any in the group are ready to do this, see "Seeking and Finding God's Forgiveness," pp. 41-42.

Study 7. Jesus the Sacrifice. Mark 14—15.

Purpose: To show that Jesus understood his death to be the sacrifice for the sins of the world and to encourage participants to accept Jesus as their Savior and Lord.

General note. This study is different from previous ones in that it covers two entire chapters. From these chapters five shorter sections have been selected for study. Because of the scope of the biblical material, the discussion itself must focus on only a few issues in each passage. Leaders should keep the content of the discussion to the following themes—the events themselves, the self-understanding of Jesus and the meaning of sacrifice. Please consult the following leader's notes; they should help you guide the group to consider the serious implications of the cross for themselves.

Group discussion. This question is designed to show just how central crosses and crucifixes have always been as symbols of the Christian faith. Their presence in significant places attests to their importance and power; their presence as costume jewelry attests to the trivialization they suffer because of human sinfulness.

Question 1. Before their famous exodus from Egypt the Israelites killed a lamb, sprinkled the blood on the doorframes of their houses so that the messenger of death would "pass over" their household and save their firstborn from death (Ex 12:1-13). They celebrated this event annually by a Passover feast. At the Last Supper, a Passover feast celebrated the night before he died, Jesus interpreted the bread as his body and the fruit of the vine as his blood; he was looking forward to his death (and his second coming [v. 25]) and to helping his disciples understand its significance as a sacrifice for sin. To interpret this historic feast as being fulfilled by his own death is, if he is wrong, an act of supreme religious megalomania.

Question 2. If Jesus knew he was going to "give his life as a ransom for many," that is, bear the sins of the world as he died, his agony makes sense. If he was wrong about this, then Socrates, who calmly faced death, is the more noble figure.

Questions 3-5. These questions bring out the irony in Mark's Gospel. Jesus is who he is charged with being—"the Christ, the Son of the Blessed One" (Mk 14:61), "the Son of Man" (14:62), and "the king of the Jews" (15:2). But the religious leaders do not realize it nor understand what these terms really mean as they apply to Jesus. For example, Jesus actually is "the Son of the Blessed One" and therefore not really guilty of blasphemy. He is king, but not of a political realm and therefore not really guilty by Roman law.

Question 6. Jesus' calm acceptance of his fate indicates that his struggle in the Garden of Gethsemane to become a sacrifice is now resolved.

Question 7. Had Jesus exercised the power he actually had, he would have denied who he was, the Savior of the world. Jesus himself said, "Whoever wants to save his life will lose it, but whoever loses his life for me will save it" (Lk 9:24). He lost his life for us but in the resurrection found it again. His death was necessary: "Without the shedding of blood there is no forgiveness" (Heb 9:22). And Peter proclaimed, "This man [Jesus] was handed over to you [the public authorities] by God's set purpose and foreknowledge" (Acts 2:23).

Question 8. Many theologians believe that this cry of dereliction from the cross is not just a quotation from Psalm 22:1, in which Jesus identifies with the agony of the psalmist and of Israel, but rather provides an insight into the spiritual realm where Jesus as God the Son finds himself separated from God the Father. It expresses the agony of dying for the sins of the world. Physical death is separation of the soul from the body. Spiritual death is the separation of the soul from God. See Romans 5:6-8 and 2 Corinthians 5:21 for further explanation of Christ's atoning sacrifice.

Question 9. The centurion may have been caught up in the emotion of the moment. But we have many reasons to believe that he was correct. Jesus claimed he could forgive sins (Mk 2:10; Lk 7:48); he made outlandish demands on those who would be disciples (Lk 6); he put himself in the place of God the Father (Lk 15:1-2, 11-31); he violated the norms of the religious leaders by making a Samaritan the hero of a story (Lk 10:30-35); he saw himself as the sacrifice for the sins of the world (Mk 10:45). If he knew he was not who he claimed to be, he was a liar who was selling a fake salvation and putting his best friends in jeopardy. Moreover, went to his death as a fool. All he would have had to do before Pilate was deny the allegations. He could have said, "Hey! You've got me all wrong. I didn't mean all those things. I was just kidding." He did not do this; he did the opposite. That Jesus was a liar makes no sense at all.

If he was wrong and didn't know it, he was not just deluded, like someone who thinks they are Napoleon, he was a very bad man. For in his teaching he misled his disciples and they misled thousands more and eventually countless millions more. Moreover, his delusions were such that they are tantamount to religious madness. But Jesus' whole life was one of keen awareness of human nature, of compassion, of sensible judgment. He did not evidence any of the characteristics of religious megalomania—paranoia and fear, the amassing of protection around himself, like David Koresh. It is far more reasonable to conclude that he really was who he claimed (and thought) he was. The centurion's conclusion became the conclusion of the early church. It was a reasonable one.

Now or Later. Our reasonable response is obvious. We should commit our lives to Jesus as Lord and Savior. If any participants are now ready to do that, you may wish to consult the section titled "Seeking and Finding God's Forgiveness," on pages 41-42.

Study 8. The Resurrection of Jesus. Luke 24:1-43.

Purpose: To consider some of the evidence for the bodily resurrection of Jesus and to encourage participants to follow Jesus.

Group discussion. This question helps give the resurrection accounts some existential credibility. The actions of those who visited the empty tomb of Jesus are psychologically credible.

General note. This short study is not sufficient to consider all the information the New Testament gives on the resurrection of Jesus. Nor is there space to consider all the objections that have been offered by skeptics. Those who want to go further or who still have some doubts should be encouraged first to read chapter 4 of John R. W. Stott's *Basic Christianity* (2nd ed. [Downers Grove: InterVarsity Press, 1971], pp. 46-60). There are a number of good books that go into detail on the resurrection. Among the best are George Eldon Ladd, *I Believe in the Resurrection of Jesus* (Grand Rapids: Eerdmans, 1975); and Gary R. Habermas and Antony G. N. Flew, *Did Jesus Rise from the Dead? The Resurrection Debate* (San Francisco: Harper and Row, 1987), a debate between two philosophers—a Christian and a well-known atheist.

The evidence for the resurrection is of six types, five of which we have noted already: (1) the empty tomb (the body is gone), (2) the position of the grave clothes, (3) the postresurrection appearances of Jesus to his followers, (4) the fulfillment of his prophecy prior to his death and (5) the consistency of the resurrection with his other claims. A fuller study of all the New Testament evidence would include a major additional item: (6) the change of the disciples from weak men to strong leaders willing to undergo persecution and death for their belief in Jesus and his resurrection. (Tradition says most of them died as martyrs.) The apostle Paul summarizes Jesus' postresurrection appearances in 1 Corinthians 15:3-7.

Question 2. Luke mentions the women because they were actually the first at the tomb. If this were not true, no Gospel writer would have invented it for the purposes of testimony. The notice of their presence helps establish the credibility of the account.

Also, if discussion about whether the women went to the wrong tomb should arise, point the group to Luke 23:55-56. The women had seen where he was buried.

Questions 4-5. Many scholars believe the "other disciple" in John 20:30 is the apostle John, the author of the Gospel or at least the eyewitness on whom the account is based. John 20:3-9 has the ring of eyewitness testimony. The grave clothes are lying in a position they would have taken if Jesus' body had been transfigured and passed through them. "The body cloths, under the weight of 100 lbs. of spices (John 19:39), once the support of the body had been removed, would have subsided or collapsed, and would now be lying flat. A gap would have appeared between the body cloths and head napkin, where his face and neck had been. And the napkin itself, because of the complicated criss-cross shape, a crumpled turban, with no head inside" (*Basic Christianity*, p. 53). Some translations do not include Luke 24:12 except in a footnote, holding that it is not in most reliable manuscripts of Luke.

Question 8. Jesus wants his disciples to know who he is and that what he has done is a fulfillment of prophecy. The disciples will be witness to what has occurred and, it is implied, when they are "clothed with power from on high" they will preach "repentance and forgiveness of sins" from Jerusalem to all nations (Lk 24:45-49).

Question 10. It is important to note that Jesus is not a "ghost" (Lk 24:37) but the same person as the one crucified. The body is no longer in the tomb; it has been transmuted but it is in some ways the same body.

Question 11. If ever a person were to be resurrected, it would be one whose life and character were like those of Jesus. Though we have not studied these passages, you might note that twice in the Gospel of Mark Jesus prophesied his death and resurrection (Mk 8:31; 10:32-34).

Question 12. Take time at the end of the session to summarize all the reasons why belief in Jesus as Lord and Savior is reasonable, I would argue, the most reasonable response that can be given to the evidence available (see general note, p. 60).

Prayer. Individuals might well wish to offer prayers of commitment to Jesus as the series of studies comes to an end.

James W. Sire is retired senior editor and campus lecturer for InterVarsity Christian Fellowship. He continues to lecture and is the author of a number of books, including The Universe Next Door: A Basic Worldview Catalog, Chris Chrisman Goes to College, Habits of the Mind: The Intellectual Life as a Christian Calling, Why Should Anyone Believe Anything at All? *and, most recently,* Naming the Elephant: Worldview as a Concept.

A Selective Bibliography of Books on Jesus

The Character of Jesus Christ

McGrath, Alister. *Understanding Jesus*. Grand Rapids: Zondervan, 1987. A basic, highly readable study of Jesus' character and work.

Sire, James W. *Why Should Anyone Believe Anything at All?* Downers Grove, Ill.: InterVarsity Press, 1994. Chapters 7-11 present a cumulative case for the Christian faith utilizing much of the same material as the present studies.

Stott, John. *Basic Christianity*. 2nd ed. Downers Grove, Ill.: InterVarsity Press, 1971. The best single book introducing the character of Christianity, primarily through its central commanding figure, Jesus.

Witherington, Ben, III. *The Christology of Jesus*. Minneapolis: Fortress, 1990. A scholarly, technical study of who Jesus understood himself to be.

———. *The Jesus Quest: The Third Search for the Jew of Nazareth*. Downers Grove, Ill.: InterVarsity Press, 1995. A scholarly assessment of recent attempts to understand Jesus in historical context.

Wright, N. T. *The Challenge of Jesus: Rediscovering Who Jesus Was and Is*. Downers Grove, Ill.: InterVarsity Press, 1999. A good first book on Jesus by a major New Testament scholar.

———. *Jesus and the Victory of God*. Minneapolis: Fortress, 1996. A profound scholarly analysis of Jesus using the methodology of the Third Quest of the historical Jesus.

———. *Who Is Jesus?* Grand Rapids: Eerdmans, 1992. A critique of three modern studies of Jesus and a presentation in brief compass of the view of Jesus developed in depth in *Jesus and the Victory of God*.

The Resurrection of Jesus

Habermas, Gary R., and Antony G. N. Flew. *Did Jesus Rise from the Dead?* Edited by Terry L. Miethe. San Francisco: Harper & Row, 1987. Records a debate between Habermas (Christian) and Flew (atheist) with presentations, rejoinders and comments by other scholars. One of the clearest, most persuasive of modern presentations of the case for the resurrection.

Ladd, George Eldon. *I Believe in the Resurrection*. Grand Rapids: Eerdmans, 1975. A scholarly analysis of the key issues surrounding the resurrection. Excellent on reconciling the various accounts in the four Gospels.

Morison, Frank. *Who Moved the Stone?* Downers Grove, Ill.: InterVarsity Press, 1958. A classic treatment by a man who set out to disprove the resurrection but changed his mind.

Wright, N. T. *The Resurrection of the Son of God*. Minneapolis: Fortress, 2003. A massive (800-plus pages) assessment of the case for the resurrection.

The Historical Reliability of the Gospels

Barnett, Paul. *Is the New Testament Reliable?* Downers Grove, Ill.: InterVarsity Press, 1986. An excellent, basic defense of the New Testament as giving a reliable account of the life and teachings of Jesus and of the early church.

Blomberg, Craig. *The Historical Reliability of the Gospels.* Downers Grove, Ill.: InterVarsity Press, 1987. A treatment more detailed than Barnett's of form criticism, redaction criticism, alleged contradictions and modern hermeneutic theory.

Dunn, James D. G. *The Evidence for Jesus.* Philadelphia: Westminster Press, 1986. An excellent introduction to the study of the differences between the synoptic accounts of the same events and teachings; the question of whether Jesus claimed to be God; the resurrection; and the early church from which the gospels emerged.

France, R. T. *Evidence for Jesus.* Downers Grove, Ill.: InterVarsity Press, 1986. Surveys the biblical and extrabiblical documents attesting to Jesus.

Marshall, I. Howard. *I Believe in the Historical Jesus.* Grand Rapids: Eerdmans, 1977. A New Testament scholar's assessment of what can be known about Jesus.

Wilkins, Michael J., and J. P. Moreland, eds. *Jesus Under Fire.* Grand Rapids: Zondervan, 1995. This collection of essays by evangelical scholars is the most basic, most accessible and most complete response to recent attempts (by the Jesus Seminar and other skeptical biblical scholars) to cast doubt on the accuracy of the biblical accounts of Jesus.

Wenham, John. *Christ and the Bible.* 2nd ed. Grand Rapids: Baker, 1984. A classic defense of the reliability of the Bible.

What Should We Study Next?

A good place to continue your study of Scripture would be with a book study. Many groups begin with a Gospel such as *Mark* (20 studies by Jim Hoover) or *John* (26 studies by Douglas Connelly). These guides are divided into two parts so that if twenty or twenty-six weeks seems like too much to do at once, the group can feel free to do half and take a break with another topic. Later you might want to come back to it. You might prefer to try a shorter letter. *Philippians* (9 studies by Donald Baker), *Ephesians* (11 studies by Andrew T. and Phyllis J. Le Peau) and *1 & 2 Timothy and Titus* (11 studies by Pete Sommer) are good options. If you want to vary your reading with an Old Testament book, consider *Ecclesiastes* (12 studies by Bill and Teresa Syrios) for a challenging and exciting study.

There are a number of interesting topical LifeGuide studies as well. Here are some options for filling three or four quarters of a year:

Basic Discipleship
Christian Beliefs, 12 studies by Stephen D. Eyre
Christian Character, 12 studies by Andrea Sterk & Peter Scazzero
Christian Disciplines, 12 studies by Andrea Sterk & Peter Scazzero
Evangelism, 12 studies by Rebecca Pippert & Ruth Siemens

Building Community
Fruit of the Spirit, 9 studies by Hazel Offner
Spiritual Gifts, 12 studies by Charles & Anne Hummel
Christian Community, 10 studies by Rob Suggs

Character Studies
David, 12 studies by Jack Kuhatschek
New Testament Characters, 10 studies by Carolyn Nystrom
Old Testament Characters, 12 studies by Peter Scazzero
Women of the Old Testament, 12 studies by Gladys Hunt

The Trinity
Meeting God, 12 studies by J. I. Packer
Meeting Jesus, 13 studies by Leighton Ford
Meeting the Spirit, 10 studies by Douglas Connelly